Book Making and Paper Making

Be Your Own Publisher

by Deborah Hufford

Capstone press

Mankato, Minnesota

Snap Books are published by Capstone Press,
151 Good Counsel Drive, P.O. Box 669, Mankato, Minnesota 56002
www.capstonepress.com

Library of Congress Cataloging-in-Publication Data
Hufford, Deborah.
  Book making and paper making : be your own publisher / by Deborah Hufford.
    p. cm. — (Snap books crafts)
  Includes index.
  ISBN 0-7368-4382-5 (hardcover)
  1. Bookbinding — Juvenile literature. 2. Papermaking — Juvenile literature.
3. Handicraft — Juvenile literature. I. Title. II. Series.
  Z271.H925 2005
  686.3 — dc22   2005006900

Summary: A do-it-yourself crafts book for children and pre-teens on making books and paper.

Editors: Thea Feldman; Deb Berry/Bill SMITH STUDIO
Illustrators: Lisa Parett; Roxanne Daner, Marina Terletsky and Brock Waldron/Bill SMITH STUDIO
Designers: Roxanne Daner, Marina Terletsky, and Brock Waldron/Bill SMITH STUDIO
Photo Researcher: Iris Wong/Bill SMITH STUDIO

Photo Credits: Cover: PhotoDisc & Richard Hutchings Photography; 4 PhotoDisc; 5 (br) Eyewire; (bl) PhotoDisc;
7 (bl) PhotoDisc; 8 & 9 PhotoDisc; 14 (br) Artville; 15 (tr) PhotoDisc; 17 Alamy Images; 21 (r) Alamy Images;
22 Tim Hicken; 25 Alamy Images; 26 Artville; 27 (br) PhotoDisc; 28 (all) PhotoDisc; 29 Dover Publishing;
32 Courtesy Deborah Hufford; All other photos Richard Hutchings Photography.

1 2 3 4 5 6 10 09 08 07 06 05

Table of Contents

Go Metric!

It's easy to change measurements to metric! Just use this chart.

To change	into	multiply by
inches	centimeters	2.54
inches	millimeters	25.4
feet	meters	.305
yards	meters	.914
ounces (liquid)	milliliters	29.57
ounces (liquid)	liters	.029
cups (liquid)	liters	.237
pints	liters	.473
quarts	liters	.946
gallons	liters	3.78
ounces (dry)	grams	28.35
pounds	grams	453.59

CHAPTER 1

A Book All Your Own

You can be a self-publisher.

Have you ever thought of writing your own book? Well, guess what? You can actually create the *entire* book yourself. You can make your own handmade paper and cover, and then put it all together. This book will show you how.

You're about to take part in the ancient craft of making paper and books. Long ago, when books were made by hand, no two were exactly alike. Your handmade book is sure to be a reflection of your own special style from cover to cover.

Paper Plant
The word "paper" comes from the word "papyrus," which is a water plant. Ancient Egyptians made some of the earliest books from it.

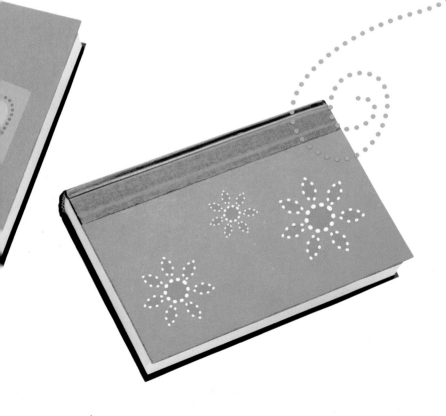

CHAPTER 2

Parts of a Book

A book is so much more than just a cover and pages.

Books come in different kinds, such as hardcovers or paperbacks, and in lots of different sizes. Even the pages of books come in many colors and thicknesses.

But all books have certain things in common. Each book has a **spine**. That's the spot where the covers and pages are bound together.

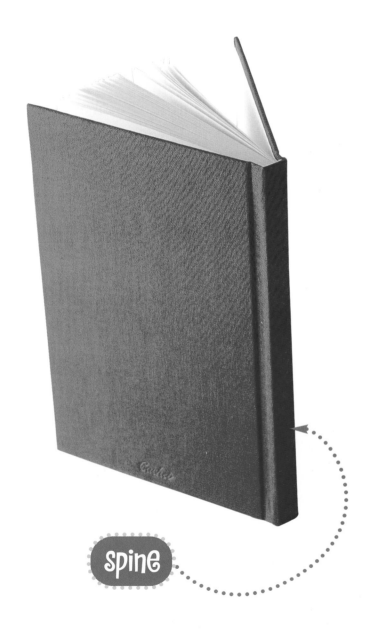

spine

binding

All books also have a **binding**. There are several different types of bindings.

Accordion-fold One long piece of paper is folded back-and-forth in small strips like an accordion.

Saddle-stitched All the pages are stapled or sewn together at the center fold.

Adhesive binding (also called **perfect binding**) Pages are glued to the inside of a squared-off spine. Most books have this type of binding.

Mechanical binding All the pages are held together by metal or plastic rings or clamps.

Everything you need to make your own handmade book can be found at your local craft store.

REMEMBER!

Safety First

Look for this box throughout the book. It's where you'll find safety tips for each project. Remember, safety first, and fun will follow.

CHAPTER 3

Mush to Magic

Paper making is simple, and the results are stunning.

Making paper is a lot like making oatmeal. It's gooey, mushy, and messy! But it's also easy and lots of fun. Once you make your first sheets of paper, you'll want to make even more, using different colors and adding materials like yarn or glitter. Most of the tools you need to make paper can be found in your own kitchen, too!

Notes About Paper

Start with white paper scraps and slowly add other colors to the blender to get the color you want. (Too many colors make gray.) Tissue paper will create a softer texture. If you want to use your paper for writing, it's a good idea to add 2 teaspoons of liquid starch to the blender. Starch keeps ink from soaking into paper.

REMEMBER!

Safety First

Always have a grown-up with you when using a blender. Never stick your fingers in it when it's on. Remember to unplug it when done.

Here's what you need

* blender
* 15 cups stamp-sized assorted paper scraps
* large mixing bowl or basin
* 8½-inch by 11-inch paper making **mold**
* dish towels
* sponge
* newspapers
* cookie sheets
* optional: 2 teaspoons liquid starch

Here's what you do

1 Lay towel flat on cookie sheet.

2 Fill blender half full with scraps, the rest with warm water.

3 Blend on low for 60 seconds until you have a smooth **pulp**.

4 Empty blender into basin and repeat Steps 1-2 twice more.

5 Push mold all the way into pulp in basin, keeping it level.

6 Gently shake mold side-to-side to spread pulp evenly.

7 Lift mold from basin, allowing water to drain completely.

8 Place mold paper side down on towel from Step 1.

9 Carefully press sponge on mold to force moisture into towel.

10 Slowly lift mold. Paper should remain on paper towel.

11 Lift towel with paper from cookie sheet and place it on newspapers.

12 Repeat steps 5-11 to make as many sheets as possible, four to five total.

13 Let paper dry 24 hours.

14 Peel paper off towels.

Paper with Pizzazz

For even more dazzling paper, add tiny stars, bits of colored yarn, glitter, sparkles, or flower petals to paper scraps in the blender.

CHAPTER 4

Bound to Please

You can hold it together.

One of the simplest bindings is the saddle-stitch. All it takes is a few staples to keep your beautiful handmade pages together. It's easy, and it really holds.

Here's what you need

* 8½-inch by 11-inch handmade paper sheets
* scissors
* stapler
* ruler
* glitter glue

Here's what you do

1 Fold each sheet in half to 8½ inches by 5½ inches.

2 Cut sheets at fold.

3 Stack sheets and fold in half again to 4¼ inches by 5½ inches.

4 Open and stack sheets with edges lined up carefully.

5 Staple sheets together three times down length of the center fold.

6 Refold pages to make book.

7 Use glitter glue to decorate the cover as you like.

My Favorite Things

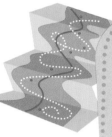

Homeward Bound

Fill your handmade book with 3½-inch by 5-inch photographs of your home, your family, even your pets. Title your book, "Home Sweet Home."

Easy-to-Make Keepsake

Accordion bindings are super easy to make. Cut a 12-inch by 3-inch strip of heavy wrapping paper. Fold it in half lengthwise, then in half again, fancy side out. Now you've got a fancy little 3-inch by 3-inch book with four inside panels.

REMEMBER!

Safety First

Never handle scissors by the blade end. Use them carefully and keep them closed when not in use.

CHAPTER 5

Be a Cover Girl

Doesn't an exciting cover make you want to open up a book?

One of the most fun things about making your own book is decorating the cover. You can use **decorative papers**, fabric, beads, charms, even photographs. Here's an idea using rhinestones or costume jewelry.

Here's what you need

* 8½-inch by 11-inch decorative paper or cloth
* 6-inch by 9-inch cardboard
* white craft glue
* **burnishing tool**
* scissors
* saddle-stitched 8½-inch by 11-inch handmade pages
* rhinestones or costume jewelry

GLUE

Here's what you do

1 Lay paper or cloth with decorated side down on work surface.

2 Fold cardboard in half to 6 inches by 4½ inches.

3 Spread glue on outer panels of cardboard.

4 Center cardboard flat across paper or cloth, glue side down.

5 Turn covered cardboard over.

6 With burnishing tool, rub out wrinkles in cloth or paper, starting from middle and working to edges.

7 Trim corners of decorative covering at an angle within ⅛ inch of each cardboard corner.

8 Glue edges of decorative covering to inside covers.

9 Let dry one hour.

10 Apply glue evenly onto spine and front pages of saddle-stitched book pages.

11 Center spine of bound pages on inside of folded cardboard and press front page down on inside front cover.

12 Use burnishing tool to smooth out wrinkles.

13 Repeat Steps 10-12 for back page and inside back cover.

14 Arrange rhinestone or costume jewelry on front cover as desired and glue into place.

Fairy Tale Frog?

What better way to decorate your fairy tale book than with a **frog knot**? This type of frog is a little corded clasp with a knot. You can buy them at fabric stores in all sorts of colors, including gold or silver. Simply glue to the front and back covers, and you have a "lock" for your book.

REMEMBER!

Safety First

Keep small crafts items such as rhinestones and jewelry away from young children and pets.

CHAPTER 6

Dazzling Diary

Make your very own journal that glitters.

You can really sparkle and shine with this very special diary covered in velvet and rhinestones. What better place to write down your thoughts than in a journal you make yourself?

Here's what you need

* 8½-inch by 11-inch piece of velvet
* 6-inch by 9-inch piece of cardboard
* scissors
* white craft glue
* burnishing tool
* transparent tape
* ruler
* white chalk pencil
* enough small rhinestones to spell out your name
* tweezers

Here's what you do

1 Follow steps 1-13 of Cover Girl craft to create velvet cover. (page 18)

2 Place piece of tape across cover at height where the bottom of the letters for your name will go.

3 Place another piece of tape 2½ inches above first piece.

4 With white chalk pencil, print your name lightly between tape pieces to create guide for rhinestones.

5 Handling rhinestones with tweezers, dot a small amount of glue on each rhinestone before gluing them evenly spaced on chalk.

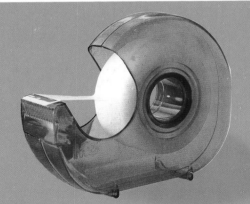

Ties That Bind

Keep the pages of your diary secret with a ribbon tie. Before gluing pages to the cover, glue a 25-inch ribbon to the inside of the cardboard cover. Lay ribbon across the inside cover so the loose ends extend 8 inches beyond each cover.

CHAPTER 7

Marvelous Mini

This tiny book is big on charm.

Sometimes the best things come in small packages. Here's a cute little book you can make with very little effort. And it's so small, you can carry it anywhere, even in your back pocket.

Here's what you need

* 8½-inch by 11-inch white paper

* 2¾-inch by 4¼-inch colored paper

* stapler

* scissors

Here's what you do

1 To create book pages, keep folding 8½-inch by 11-inch white paper in halves until you have a booklet about 2⅛ inches by 2¾ inches.

2 Fold 2¾-inch by 4¼-inch colored paper in half to make book cover.

3 Lay folded white papers on cover sheet so that center folds line up.

Up Against a Wall?
Use floral, striped, or plaid wallpaper for your cover paper! You can get free scraps and samples at some paint stores.

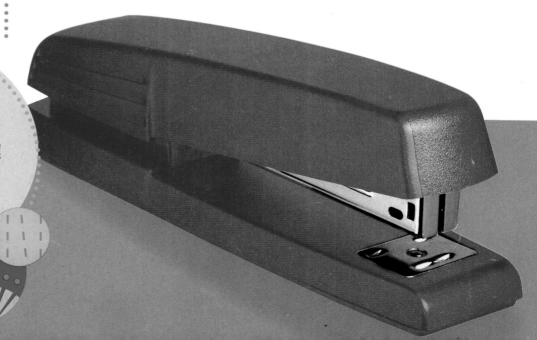

4 Staple cover and folded pages together along center folds.

5 Cut open top, bottom, and right edges of folded white pages to "free" them.

Fast Facts

Written in Stone

Book making goes back 4,000 years. Some early books were printed on stone and clay. Others were printed on plants or animal skins such as sheepskin. It wasn't until 1843 that paper started being made from wood.

Rags to Riches

In Europe in the 1400s, rags were used to make paper pulp. Rags became so valuable, countries started wars over them. England even passed laws that wouldn't let people bury the dead in cotton or linen. They wanted the cloths to be used for making paper!

Just Your Type

In the mid-1400s, Johann Gutenberg invented a printing press with "movable type." With this new press, books could be printed in mass numbers. Before Gutenberg's invention, books were created by copying them by hand or printing them from hand-carved blocks of wood.

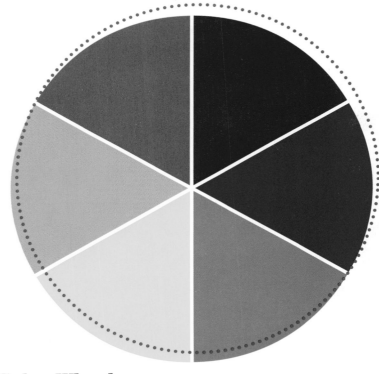

Color Wheel

When making paper and books, color is key. This wheel shows how colors work with each other. The colors next to each other work together in harmony. Colors opposite each other have a stronger effect when used together because they have more contrast.

29

Glossary

binding (BINDE-ing) the way the cover and pages of a book are held together

burnishing tool (BURN-ish-ing TOOL) tool made of wood, plastic, or bone with curved, flattened end used for smoothing paper, cloth, and bindings

decorative paper (DEK-ur-uh-tiv PAY-pur) paper that come in many colors, styles, and patterns

frog knot (FROG NOT) a type of clasp made from fancy cord and usually used on Chinese clothing as buttons

liquid starch (LIK-wid STARCH) a liquid that stiffens paper or cloth

mold (MOHLD) screen-like device used to sift pulp in papermaking

publisher (PUHB-lish-ur) a person or company who makes and distributes books

pulp (PUHLP) soft, soggy mass of water and fibers used to make paper

rhinestones (RYNE-stohnz) fake gems and diamonds made of plastic, glass, or crystal

spine (SPYNE) the "backbone" of a book, where pages and cover are bound together

texture (TEKS-chur) the way something feels

Read More

Diehn, Gwen. *Making Books That Fly, Fold, Wrap, Hide, Pop Up, Twist, And Turn.* New York: Sterling Publishing, 1999.

Haab, Sherri. *Making Mini Books.* Palo Alto, California: Klutz, 2002.

Liddle, Matthew. *Make Your Own Book.* Philadelphia: Running Press Book Publishers, 1993.

Morris, Ann and Peter Linenthal. *The Bookmaking Kit.* San Francisco: Chronicle Books, 2001.

Internet Sites

FactHound offers a safe, fun way to find Internet sites related to this book. All of the sites on FactHound have been researched by our staff.

Here's how

1. Visit *www.facthound.com*

2. Type in this special code **0736843825** for age-appropriate sites. Or enter a search word related to this book for a more general search.

3. Click on the **Fetch It** button. FactHound will fetch the best sites for you!

About the Author

Deborah Hufford was a staff writer for *Country Home* and the former editor of *Country Handcrafts* magazine, which included a regular craft column called "Kids' Korner." She was also the crafts editor for *McMagazine,* a magazine created for McDonald's Corporation. Most recently she served as the associate publisher for two of the country's leading craft magazines, *Bead & Button* and *Dollhouse Miniatures*, as well as a book division of crafts titles.

Index